Threshold

Crab Orchard Series in Poetry

OPEN COMPETITION AWARD

Threshold

JENNIFER RICHTER

Crab Orchard Review

&

Southern Illinois University Press

CARBONDALE AND EDWARDSVILLE

13   12   11   10   4   3   2   1

The Crab Orchard Series in Poetry is a joint publishing venture of Southern
Illinois University Press and *Crab Orchard Review.* This series has been made
possible by the generous support of the Office of the President of Southern
Illinois University and the Office of the Vice Chancellor for Academic Affairs
and Provost at Southern Illinois University Carbondale.

Crab Orchard Series in Poetry Editor: Jon Tribble
Open Competition Award Judge for 2009: Natasha Trethewey

Library of Congress Cataloging-in-Publication Data
Richter, Jennifer, 1969–
Threshold / Jennifer Richter.
        p. cm. — (Crab Orchard series in poetry)
ISBN-13: 978-0-8093-2965-6 (pbk. : alk. paper)
ISBN-10: 0-8093-2965-4 (pbk. : alk. paper)
ISBN-13: 978-0-8093-8567-6 (ebook)
ISBN-10: 0-8093-8567-8 (ebook)
I. Title.
PS3618.I364T47 2010
811'.6—dc22   2009027037

Printed on recycled paper. ♻

The paper used in this publication meets the minimum requirements of
American National Standard for Information Sciences—Permanence of Paper
for Printed Library Materials, ANSI Z39.48-1992. ∞

For my mother and father,

and for Tony Vallone:

my first teachers

There are years that ask questions

and years that answer.

— ZORA NEALE HURSTON

Contents

4

5

6

Acknowledgments

Grateful acknowledgment is made to the editors of these publications, in which the following poems first appeared:

Calyx: "Everywhere the Earth Is Opening"
The Carolina Quarterly: "Name One Thing You Love"
Cloudbank: "The Damp Grass Catches You Wherever You Lie Down," "Persephone Returns"
Crab Orchard Review: "In the Air," "They Name Each Other Jesus"
The Denny Poems 1997–1998: "The Fifth Element"
A Fierce Brightness: Twenty-five Years of Women's Poetry: "Everywhere the Earth Is Opening"
The Healing Muse: "First Words"
Mānoa: "After the Mud Bath"
The Missouri Review: "The Day You Choose," "Fairy Tale: The Doctor," "Recovery," "Recovery 3," "Recovery 6: The Last Word," "She Asks about Death, Then Draws"
Open City: "Click," "Magic Word," "Recovery 2: Turn Away Your Eyes and It'll Fly," "Recovery 4," "Relapse"
Poetry: "Annunciation"
Whetstone: "Prayer for the Hanoi Man Who Waits for Breakdowns on His Block"
"You Were Born to Be Mine, See, Why Even Fight It" was chosen for the Tupelo Press Poetry Project and was published on their website.

For their enthusiastic, enduring belief in me and my work, I'm grateful to Bruce Weigl, Eavan Boland, Simone DiPiero, Kenneth Fields, and Peter Sears. I'm grateful to Natasha Trethewey for holding my manuscript in her hands and deciding, This one. I'm deeply thankful to Jon Tribble, who's had faith in this book for years; to Barb Martin, Bridget Brown, Robert Carroll, Jennifer Fandel, Erin Kirk New, Wayne Larsen, and SIU Press for their careful and gorgeous work; to David Keplinger and Colleen Morton Busch, every day; to Vernon Bowlby, for bringing me back; to my dear friends and family; and to my dazzling children and my extraordinary husband, Keith Scribner: the three reasons I never gave up.

1

Threshold:

where mothers prop themselves, welcoming, waving, mostly waiting. You are a frame your child passes through, the safest place to stand when the shaking starts. You brace yourself. He draws you like this, arms straight out, too stick-thin but the hands are perfect, splayed like suns, long fingers, the hands he draws for you are huge. Thresh, hold: separate the seeds, gather them back. In his pictures you all come close to holding hands, though the fingers of your family never touch; you're in the middle of all this reaching.

Magic Word

They taught you only one. Only one works in the real world, one
that sometimes gets you what you want. The others—long invented
commands crowded with vowels—you kept to yourself. Your childhood
nights wandered through woods; the downstairs clink and shush of
company turned to the chirp and flutter of birds that led you through.
You knew a shadowed door was hidden in the tallest oak; you knew
the word to swing it open and go.

Years, and you're back. The forest is denser, darker than you
remembered. Pain has branched through your body and rooted you.
The wrens waiting in the clearing up ahead are your children. You want
to be blinking back into their bright light but nothing you say works.
All the shadows are you. You're collapsing like a kid, begging. You're
back there. You're asking.

Spring, and It Starts to Snow

The day you said *Okay, I'll go,* your mother packed your bag. To fold
the shoulders in, she held your flattened shirts against her chest. You
both knew you'd need none of them. Your IV pole stands stable on its
shiny star of wheels. You watch the weather like you're on a trip. The
sky is gauze. Your view: a little row of tulips that deer have finished off.
It's hard, sometimes, to live. With one hand now, your mother holds the
tray; the other slides your bed rail down. She tilts the milk, guides your
lips. Years ago, you thought that you knew pain. You held your breasts.
You thought: I'll nurse my daughter one more month, then I can be done.
Your mother stares into the falling snow. *You never know*, she says and
grins. You close your eyes. Years ago, you waited till your daughter slept,
and then you sobbed.

*Ask Yourself Whether You Are Having Children
to Be Loved, or to Love*

You can say it now, he's four, he has a younger sister, now you can say you
wanted a girl first. Wanted the strange changing body in yours to emerge
as yours.

You can say it because what happened? Today he gave you acorns, two
tiny ones attached at the caps. This is between the two of you. He knows
you keep it all. He knows your body better than anyone.

Once he picked a daffodil, dunked the bloom in his bucket and watered
your name across the hot driveway. He didn't mean for you to see, he
crouched down and blew to make you go away. Say it, you can say it now.
It's like lovers: all the loyalties and letdowns.

You Are Time to Wake Up

You have been sick for years. You have been sick since Monday. Your
son confuses weeks and months, forgets the names of days. You are his
measure of time sliding by. He's old enough to know the one you were
before. Now he watches you twist up your lipstick and asks you *How long
have you had that?* He asks *Is it the weekend?* All eyes are on the lipstick,
its slow spiral down. He says *Now you look like someone else.* He loves
you and he says it out loud. You looked at him like this when he was
born: Here was the one you'd been waiting for. Here was the one who,
after all this time, you didn't even recognize.

Today Is a Capital M

Open your eyes, and you have a slow count of five to be someone else. Then—the pain's awake. You squint into it, as if the sun's already up. You have a full glass always on the counter and you rush: past the robe you've worn thin at the back, past the light switch, toilet, thermostat, kettle. Today is a capital M. You open the little plastic hatch. (In your purse, you know these pills by touch: bullet capsules with seams, slick tablets you swallow with just spit, foil rectangles with nicks where you should rip, and small half-moons crumbled and rattling. No safety cap so you can screw it with one hand, in traffic.) Eat immediately or you're dizzy, clutching the counter, and today you can't go back to bed. Today you need to get dressed. You'll walk funny in your pants because you're used to sweats; you'll welcome the gown they give you. Your closet doors stick shut, then *whoosh*—you flinch—cold blows straight into your face. It's the air the doctors push in from the hall when they arrive already talking. Their mouths are wounds. Their mouths are winds. You feel the cold when they come. You stand and smile and shake.

Recovery

Health means Nowhere to hide. For weeks you will fear the phone, the
calendar, the life that, for seasons, sustained your pain. Your children
will grab your hands and run you through the rooms you've missed; your
husband will pat the sheets next to him and wait.

But here come the night nurses now, fresh back from the steel box
that warms the blankets. Here comes one with her flashlight, eyeing
the plastic bag hung above your head, following it down to your arm's
irritated site—this last night won't hurt. When she shakes out the
blanket she's brought, one wing rushes through your room. You slide into
your warm white tent. If you speak up, you're not just talking to your
body when you say *Enough.*

Recover means, of course, Cover again. Put on another layer. Even if the
pain stays, it's not exposed. Maybe you'll quit being so cold.

2

Fairy Tale: The Doctor

You've been waiting your whole life for this man. Today you have been
granted access. He has prepared this room for you. You hear him in the
hall. You sit up straight. Last night you practiced what you'd say. In the
end you expect a change. One door down he booms *Knock knock who's
there I am: your doctor.* To the stranger one door down he asks *How are
we?* Through the wall, the softer voice is either asking many questions,
or pleading. You will wait your whole life for this man. There are often
two versions of the same story. Here mice turn into footmen, wringing
their hands.

Putting the Baby to Sleep: Nine Tries

Oh my God, what am I

That these late mouths should cry open

—SYLVIA PLATH, "Poppies in October"

1

Once upon a time a woman walked with her children through a grove of trees. When she stopped at one of the madrones, the children scuffed on ahead, kicking up stiff scrolls of bark. The smooth trunk dipped into navels, and the place where her palm rested felt like a belly, a breast. Now her children were gone. When she tried to call for them she couldn't—these two who were just learning language together had carried all the words with them. So she stood still in the silence and hoped her son and daughter would come to her. Soon enough they did, of course, singing, scuffing, not looking at her, not lost at all.

2

The way to finally
get rid
of this pain:
on tiptoes.
I call it
putting the baby
to sleep,
my neurologist
tells me:
you have
to back out
slowly
and quietly.
Make sure
the baby
doesn't stir.

3

From the top, the skull on film is a perfect cup, a thin-rimmed bowl, the brain a rain-rippled stone. Silent. Uncapped like that, why is there no black blot, no hole to explain my months of drawing the shades, living out of the light? Look, I might have said once, isn't it amazing, your own brain? It's everything we need. How can it be everything we need? From the side, my skull in black and white could be anyone. I mean anyone dead.

4

This is the time
we'd be bringing
another child
home. Instead,
the ache comes
and stays. I'm
dropping them off,
driving home
to nap in Luke's
cold bed
or buying Chloe
a doll for Christmas:
not the eyelashed
blinking kind,
a wrinkly pink
newborn.
Baby, she
calls it,
leaves it
in the box.

5

At bedtime I go back there:
August nights in Hanoi,
families sleep on the sidewalks.
Their intimately tangled bodies—
I want my kids
that close, thin
nets draped over
their faces like spirits.

6

In this time, it has become winter.
The leaves, my language: all gone.
My husband's finger shrinks from his ring.

7

The brain has a memory for pain;
I will be more susceptible
to this in the future. My friend
sews me a flannel pillow,
spoons in heaps of flaxseed
and millet. Good as bread,
its grains and weight, its warmth
that stays so long on my neck
I move it to my belly,
curl around it as it cools.

8

In this time, he's learned
to stop at three: my son
who used to make a ladder
of his E's now knows
three rungs, one pole
end his name. He's worried
and he won't sleep,
so after five days
I say I'm okay.
He won't sleep
till we wrap him up
and carry him to the driveway
to see the stars, lift him
up to kiss the moon
where he says someday
he wants to live.
We praise his little ladders,
so few steps
to all that space.
Does he know, now,
that's all I am?

9

She says *Now tell me a* true *story.*

I am nobody I have known yet in me
Two children in school, first day
I am crying in the driveway
Garden blackened and hanging, claws of frost
Two poppies with no business blooming
No sun no rain no sway
Two poppies tall on their stalks
I bring one inside and it dies
Two because I learn slowly
Sometimes you get an answer back
Two loud mouths saying *Now*
Poppies are everything you think
They are where we open
Healing is the black seeded center
What you think of first as the wound
You go in deep
Not the light at your back but the darkness
Your child asleep

Recovery 2: *Turn Away Your Eyes and It'll Fly*

Pain stands you behind glass. A curiosity, a diagnosis, you inspire in everyone a circus of speculation. You are changed; they squint to see the measured you who speaks in meter, who doesn't grimace and grind her teeth like some beast.

Sometimes a flash of wings will crash into your glass then slump, shitting and shivering, staring, standing, now opening its mouth, its throat. The silence streaming out: a sound its loves aren't meant to hear. They'd hurt. You won't ever tell. This will happen to you again.

3

Persephone Returns

In the yard, the bulbs are coming up: the earth has holes again where
shoots pierce through. The girl is back; she's locked her bedroom door.
Once she used to tell her mother everything; she used to whine *Come
with me.* On the line her mother pins up sheets; she's reaching for the
gods: what now? She knows the one her daughter sneaks out nights to
meet. Each time Persephone returns, there is more of him in her. In
every sheet, he's here: his shadow moving through them. She calls her
daughter's name. The girl won't wake. In her bed is grit from his river.

Everywhere the Earth Is Opening

After eight dry months of dirt,
this morning glowed all grass
and my pomegranate bush
finally boasted its knobby fruit.

Though mistakenly called apple
in that first search for skin
through the vine, I mean
another myth, another love altogether:

I mean that fruit that draws a curtain of earth
between mothers and daughters.
First light, I stooped low to the ground
but there were no deals to make

—she is dying, my mother's mother,
and won't make it till I touch down—
so I plucked each red bead
and littered them on the lawn, left them.

Mother, how can you possibly be next?
Everywhere the earth is opening
into slits that smell alive
and, between them, blooms.

Follow me, step into the soil.
Forget the fields. Let the others look.
We will always be daughters
and the dazzling seeds go down easy.

After the Mud Bath

We rose from the earth headfirst:
faces, necks, shoulders, outstretched arms.
With her eyes the attendant pointed
our black-crusted bodies toward the shower,
said with her eyes *You are nothing new.*
Millions of years fell in clumps at our feet,
wet volcanic ash streaking
a thin gray slip on our skin
until we used our hands, my mother
and I facing each other in our bodies
I once willed the same.
She knew she was touching where others had been
and with both hands she swept my breasts clean.
I knew part of her that year
had stilled like ash in thick tubs.
Men and their hands slid toward the drain
until water was the only sound
and we had nothing to do with anyone else.
She was taking me back into her.
I felt my heart just below
the skin, our skin free of this
heavy earth. Then under the spigot
she parted her legs. Black like silt
rushed to the tile: sudden
flood of what once burned.

Laying on Hands

Everybody he loves is a gesture, so that when his brother at the fence last night
wrapped his arms around himself and hugged, head bowed, he meant Mama.
Then the word: two palms together, flat out in prayer: Dead.

His window is a square of yard and fence—prison yard, spiked fence.
Brothers, cousins, lovers stand for hours on the free side
and use their hands to tell the news. In case he's looking.

And he's always looking, unless he's with me. Once a week
he shows me his poems and though my tag says Teacher I tell him
Don't change a thing. He makes me see how much my poems lie.

On his arms the bones show through. And on his fingers,
the tops of his hands, blue inked bones set apart like boxcars
run the length of his tracked skin. It's not like looking inside him.

He says the tattoos are something he asked for—
and these years at County. El Paso County Jail. *Injustice,* he says,
is when you get what you didn't ask for.

We've missed a week. Last time, I was seamless. Now, my scar,
he can't bear it—sees me as walking Good and he's wild
that he can't protect me, not from the streets, not from my body gone wrong—

says I didn't ask to have part of me cut out and he's had it
with bad news so before the guard rushes up he puts his palms to my belly,
thumbs hooked, fingers splayed, with his hands he makes a bird,

bird of bones that flies as he's pulled away, makes the word
he's always waiting for, fluttering at the fence,
his child brother cousin lover paroled escaped got out somehow Gone.

Annunciation

And the angel left her.
—LUKE 1:38

*

Last spring my neighbor
who thinks babies are the answer
to everything said *You must
be pregnant.* Weeks, my low ache
no doctor could explain was
maybe something reproductive?
The day I stripped down
for the ultrasound, you and I
were already grieving with the idea
of us alone, family of two,
when the screen swept green
and came up with nothing.
Finally, surgery took what I
could live without. But by then I had
believed my neighbor, felt my breasts
grow heavy with milk, and carried
the new low weight in my hips.
At home where she was waiting
at the fence for me, she hollered
I'm due in December, stretching
her shirt tight across her belly.

*

Any day now. My neighbor paces
her yard then digs deep holes in the earth

to get her body and her baby moving.
She loves babies, loves less what they become:

the youngest is always her favorite
and why not, who's to say how to live

in the wake of the angel, her husband
gone before the third was born, the first

already growing into his father's face
and crossing streets alone.

Oh month of miracles, bless us,
deliver us from darkness.
By nine each night her kids
leave her for sleep; each night
she waits for them to need her.
Angels must be what
we wake to (faith: our way
of asking them to stay),
the oldest at her bedside
now, on his lips a dream
he can't explain, and you,
reaching across the sheets
for me, dream of child
in your breath, you
who held me last spring
when I woke from surgery's dark;
you, all bright light and good news.

Name One Thing You Love

Write about what you love, I say—
because to write about what they know could cost them
more time in these hallways locked at both ends.

I say *Name one thing* so Tony says *Speed*—
testing me—I shoot him the eye
so he says *PLANES, man, I'm talking PLANES,*
150 miles an hour at touchdown. No shit. I love that.

He's never been on one, but knows a plane's windows
aren't like all the ones here: big squares, spray-painted white
on the outside, all his ghosts shoved up to stare.

They can come with one bottle of shampoo:
got to be clear as glass. No tricks.
XL on their backs, Property of San Mateo Juvenile Hall.
All of them goofy in their bodies.

I'm thinking love because hate is the same old story.
And because last night you leaned into me, said *Lover, be my wife.*

I ask Tony what he might see from a plane.
He says *Doin' time is like shootin' down a kite.*
That's no answer, and he knows it.
But I get the point: drop it.

I'm thinking love, thinking falling

because they want that poem again,
can't get enough of that girl sucked out of the hatch
at 35,000 feet, wailing, praying,

creaming the clouds in her long fall,
beginning to be something
that no one has ever been and lived through:
on the tape the poet's long drawl
the only twenty minutes I've ever seen them still, and still
the girl stripping on the way down, touching herself—

Mr. Speed says *It wouldn't take that long.*

Six months or more: dark blue shirts. They mean trouble.
The youngest boys, first offenders, with the girls in orange:
they're talking days, a week maybe.
Green and maroon: middlemen.

Sweetest are the drug dealers—I know them when they look me
   in the eye
and speak, polite, smooth-talking their way to my bones.
Fiancé: a word they would use. Flouncy, Frenchy.
Everyone else talks like firecrackers strung on a long lit fuse.

End of every class: line-up, pencil-check.
One missing—nobody goes anywhere.
It's Tony, he's writing, his brain fisted around something,
his forehead a landslide bunched up on his brows:

I love people but I'm scared to death of them.

I'm thinking me, those years I wouldn't be touched.
Yes, I said last night. *Of course.*

Recovery 3

Now you can't break down. The experts have sent you home. People are waiting for you. Tonight your husband pulls in the driveway, kills the engine, drops his hands to his lap and sits staring. When he finally comes to the door, he's like a relative that resembles him slightly. You take his coat, you feed him. You lead him to bed. You can't break. Once on a trip, your parents put your pillow in the backseat and said when the sky turned light you'd arrive. You woke. Night. The hood was open. The heater was silent. Your father: silent. When you set off, you didn't expect to have to stop in the darkness. You never expected to stay there.

4

Kept from Her

Like this? she asks. Lying at my side, my daughter wants to know with
how much force she used to nurse. My shirt has fallen open; she takes
my skin in her lips. She's five. Each night, another question. Why did we
ever stop? she hasn't thought of yet. My son was easy: he gave me time
to try and fill him, then one day pulled away. With her, the truth: I'd had
enough. I kept her from my lap so she'd forget about my breasts. She
thrashed her head from side to side; she reached. Now she won't let go.
Forgive me. You reached and screamed; you mouthed the air for me.

For Chloe, Whose Name Means "Profusion of Blooms"

In the cloud-and-mud mountains of North Vietnam,
the flowers running the ridges are children:
Sapa mothers crown their babies with bright hats
so the spirits soaring overhead pass by,
mistaking them for blooms.

In the Air

The neighbor knocked when the snow
and the seventh newspaper
piled up, and the man inside
opened his home as he does now
for the one reporting live, says he
and his family are opening their bodies
to this season, to the holy ghost, says
there's plenty to live on in the air
so they sit and wait for the spirit to fill them.
They haven't eaten in days and the studio
doctor cuts in, warns us
against this and shakes his head
so my son shakes his, pleased
to practice the skeptical gesture though
already he's a believer in what
he can't see: the hidden block,
my face behind a cloth, imaginary
water in a cup he holds to my lips.
He palms each of the flat faces
on screen, camera slowly panning
the family that in months could be us
lined up on the couch: mother,
father, son, daughter who waits
in me, breathing the air in my blood.
The anchorman stacks his papers, smirks
and of course it's crazy, all of it:
why something like birth should work,
why certain days give way to grace—
Luke walks up humming
to say his kettle's ready, offers me
the small empty cup and saucer.
He's made it clear there's always more—

Plenty, he might say someday—
so I take it to my lips again and again.
He palms my belly, his sister
still in her world of water;
when I drink, he waits and watches,
his mouth, like mine, opening.

The Fifth Element

Here we live with only four,
and air instead of wood.

There they know air is no home, air cannot burn
and heat a pot to cook the rice. So: wood.

Humid, visible, heavy: Hanoi's air is water.
The air of Dong Xuan Market, swimming with fish.

And street air: *pho* steam rising, the wet
sizzle of meat as it's dropped in raw.

Fiery midafternoons, Hotel Viet Long, no air
so we'd strip, blow on each other.

I mean, we were on fire: one element.
Incense smoke, air, wood-scent.

On young wood, men rise from the dirt
into air. Scaffolding: bamboo and twine.

Children walk the pavement as on coals,
hoping to be healed. Earth. Fire.

Water buffalo: what element?
Color of rain sky, tossing its heavy head.

Water: to drink it, boil it—turn some of it
into air, an element we recognize.

Tiny coals, the woman's betel-black teeth,
her laughter a crackle of fire.

But the fifth—what else
kept me alive there? Not rice,

rice is the earth, raked into one thin sheet
and drying on the road.

Not stone, stone is part water:
the women beat them both to wash our clothes

while we'd wait, naked, our bags emptied.
Once, you left me after love to stand

at the window—what was it you saw, heard,
that got you glowing, rushing back?

The ring of bikes, the gong of a funeral
waking the gods, spoons on the lips

of soup pots, *metallic,* yes, the fifth one:
metal or gold. Practical and precious:

the golden light you brought back to bed,
all the days you bathed me in the iron-ringed tub,

all the scrap they've saved from the war,
tracks for tanks now fences and roofs,

the element worth risking a life
in the deep green fields still mined.

First Words

Child, you were light all at once.
You did not tunnel toward the bright
world waiting; from a small slit
like a crimp in the blinds, they pulled you
from me and held you to the sky,
held you crying, held you shining,
your fair skin lit from the inside,
your hair one huge fine red flame.
Luke, luminous, we chose the name
before we were sure of you
and since you came, our usual season
of rain has stayed away. Today,
sun strong at our backs, day of the year's
longest night, you sit on my lap,
wave your arm in the most deliberate
gesture I've seen, follow the spread
of your fingers across the floor
and just like that add shadows
to what you already know.
Already, you have a songlike voice
though it has taken four months
and this moment to coax my first words.
Strange, this turning from you to the page,
so I wait until I hear the poem
whole in my head. Luke: the one
who found words for that one birth,
that famous star. In this season,
son, you live in holy mouths.
When you were born, the doctors
held you up with arms raised,
and all our faces tilted to the place

blessings come from, and names,
and the first words, and light. Luke,
luminous, your hand in the air is a star;
on the floor our shadow is still one body.

Ode to the Bones

Shadowless tree
inside me
you hide your light;
only once
I went looking
for you. On the screen
it seemed I had swallowed
a skeleton, a nurse
counted the tiny
milk pearls
strung along
my baby's back.
Oh bones,
how many of you
haven't we found?
In Quang Ngai
province, the hills
great and bare
are mothers desperate
to keep you.
Settled in the soil,
rice-white
and quiet as mines,
you outlast us.
Over a bomb crater
now a lake
stocked with fish,
a woman leans
to reach her line
and her sheer catch
she holds to the light.
Woman started with you.

You are the steeple
of this woman's spine,
you are what's left
to hold of her husband,
you are the fish's
bone-fan body.
Your one smooth
song says *Heal*.
She'll take it in
later, easing
out through her lips
one thin rib.

Prayer for the Hanoi Man Who Waits
for Breakdowns on His Block

One like him on every block, a man
who crouches by his tray of parts: gears,
plugs, bolts, sprockets, cogs, his greasy
jewels displayed on slick black oil.
But this is for the man on Hang Bai Street,
the block before the lake—the man who looked
away when I walked past, who dropped his eyes
to hide the war of scars his body is.
Oh God, so much to fix. Give him, once
a day at least, a woman at his feet; give him
what it takes to fix her limping bike.
Forgive us all. Make his next world one
that doesn't always fall apart around him.

Recovery 4

Each day you lay a few more things on the lawn. The way the neighbors
pare down. The dozens of wobbling ladders in the grass: these are your
doctor's long reports. The boxes labeled "Fragile": your nights awake.
Your pills are the shoes, lined up in rows. A camper trailer on blocks:
the public shape your grief has taken.

Your husband isn't sure he likes what's left. For years he was your shield:
returning calls, muting the news, handing his heaviness to others. Your
reactions have been flat as cut grass. Now you're striding through the
empty rooms, swinging open doors. You're sweating. You don't want help.
You're pressing past him, seeing at the last minute what you can't part
with and rushing to it, out there.

5

The Damp Grass Catches You Wherever You Lie Down

Sun in June: what everybody expects. You wake up warmed by it, the bright half of bed your husband rolls from to hold you. Upstairs, the children's first stirs could be winds blowing slowly; soon the sky is your name, over and over again. Now louder. They are waiting for you to wipe night from their eyes. Each of your loves you have fed with your breasts, though now you are walking out, you are lying back in the grass, you are no one they know. This morning the moon, too, hovers huge. Most won't notice. You're wanting a woman again. You know about small voices getting louder. Inside you is a darkness where she hides; inside your night she shines. Above your roof she's barely there, thin as a slip, the haze of a face.

Some Run

Just to fake a breeze, some run
on days this hot. I drive my kids
to sleep in the car's AC,
six loops around our town,
six times past the phone-pole
posters that hit me hard
as glimpsing highway wreckage:
JESSE GONZALES
Please Call Home Collect.
A mother knows to leave her plea
at that. She wrote the name she chose,
then retraced every letter.
Once before in heat like this
I saw such desperation:
dead horses stiff-kicking the sky
as I drove some Costa Rican road.
Their grimaced lips pulled back
made me never want to look again.
I hear my children's drowsy mouths;
in sleep they lean their heads together.
Safe. Say this was a legend;
each dead horse would branch
into birches, lure the lost child
to their shade. The earth would shrink
down to us in our car,
as it does, our windows all glare
from rounding the closest star.
Some run. Some drive;
this is the way I'd search for mine
if they were lost, the way a horse
gallops a corral in scared circles.

———

What Is My Body Without You?

My son's pajamas unsnapped
on the floor: small husk
of his body relaxing on its back,
legs and sleeves still filled
with his rush. This part of him
hasn't outgrown my arms
and sometimes lets me lift
him up our steep stairs,
carry him to bed and pull
his shade against the gray
thin winter sky like milk
my daughter wakes up wanting.
In the last days of lifting her
to my breast, I fill her less
than the air already gone
from my son's flat shape.
Twice like that I have lain back,
the doctor opening me
along the same clean seam.
Each time I was watching:
with a few tugs the child
was out, naked and heading
toward other hands, each child
cut loose before I knew it.

They Name Each Other Jesus

Through news-flickering rooms again tonight they orbit
in tight fists, ravage each other with squalls.

They have brought us from bed to the moon
making soapstone of our still bodies and from here

we can see it all: stroke that sweeps away dinner plates,
clock and cross above their sink,

TV map of many suns and then the featured man
who holds with two fingers a spoon's neck

and stares till it moves, the round face
arcing up then back exactly like yours above mine.

We will not touch again until they do, our neighbors
becoming your father working his words in predictable loops,

your bead-fingering mother who taught you faith
in repetition: the clock's arms meeting once an hour,

the similar voices of sex and rage when after words
bodies lace together like prayer hands.

Fog prowls the ridge in this grounded world
below stars in the night run riot.

Window-lit proof of houses spills down the ravine.
They name each other Jesus with their screams.

Set a Place at Your Table for Grief

You think this bowl

is for you. It's not.

This bowl is your womb

washed clean, it's the lid

of your empty head lifted,

it's the hollow of your breast.

This is about emptying.

She's already two.

She will be your last.

To Gather Back the Body

My daughter opens
buds before
they've bloomed,
a careful peek
into the sweet
secret center
the way I'd love
a woman. You.
I'd bend above
your chest,
breathe in.
I'm more sure
of how to hold
your breasts
than how
to raise a daughter.
The poppies part
their wrinkled flashy
skirts for her,
she strokes
their hairy
leaves. I love
her for choosing
the strongest stalks
in the yard, all
that back-talking
orange grace.
When she
sees me,
she stops.

How close
can I
ever go?
I want you.
Give me
mystery—
what I've lived
is why I worry:
she's just
like me.
She licks
her pollen
fingertips.
You and I
would lift
each other's
milk-rinsed
breasts to share
their weight
of many mouths.
I'd lie along
your spine's
long stem,
stretch to reach
your belly
and imagine
it's mine,
wide with the child.
I'd gather back
my body.
I'd be one
more time
two women
at once.

Recovery 5: Now What Do You Do?

The pain is like a child. You marked it first in days, then months. Now years. Your son is five. Today he drops your hand a block before his school. He sprints up the stairs and disappears. Certain doors, you crave to be behind again. You'd sit at his small desk, make a new picture of what you'd do when you grew up. You'd sit at his small desk and start over. In the bright buzz of the o.r., everyone believed you would heal. Your nurse was reading the beeps on a screen: *Your numbers look good,* she said. *You have a good heart.* She swung the doors shut. She held your hand. Your son, when he sees you, drops his books and comes running. *You'll be fine,* she said. *You'll do good.*

6

You Were Born to Be Mine, See, Why Even Fight It

I'm good at making hearts. Seven years ago inside me I made yours. Bedtime tonight, you pull me close and whisper; you ask me how to spell "admirer." You don't ask why I wipe my eyes or why your father's out again or why each night we think our voices rising down the hall don't keep you up. A boy your age once hid this in my desk: "Now I'm positive I love you." The first time you wrote "love," you handed it to me. But this new word, in your careful printing, I know I'll never see. Once I held you in my lap and showed you how to cut a heart. You tried and tried. Yours looked like a little mouth, surprised. You held mine in your hands. *Yes,* I said. *You can have it.*

Relapse

Last year there were plenty of apples. And not wormy and chewed through. Now the tree is budding again, and your husband chooses today to prune the shoots. Then he hacks below the trunk's thick knots. Your daughter cries above the noise. Falling to the driveway are fists of gnarled bark. Wind lifts a few petals; today, another of your experts shrugged her shoulders. Everyone's sick of your story. At least all spring your kids will look at this instead of you. Look at this. The truth is, you looked around all winter for something safe to damage.

Click

There was no fire but everything beyond our back fence glowed. The sky
was sirens: red, alive. Her father cut the grass that day then waited out
the light and took his life. From my window in the dark I watched their
crowded kitchen move. The girl ran screaming *God* into the yard past
branches planted at her birth. The cardinal woke and sang What here?
What here? Line up our families before: we matched. The girl's arms thin
as mine to pass a tiny broken eggshell through the fence. The red one
singing birdie birdie birdie in his bandit mask thought only of himself.
The gun hung on a nail behind her father's clothes. She wasn't meant
to know. When the girl returned to Sunday school, the teacher startled,
Oh! Hello! Let us start over, the teacher said. The girl refused to bow her
head. The rest of us stared at the floor; we mumbled together *Our father.*
The night he died I hid her in my house. I closed my closet door until it
clicked. That night I was afraid of her.

She Asks about Death, Then Draws

You woke knowing you'd left her. You had fallen asleep reading to her, and you woke layered in paper. She'd lain herself on your legs, making drawings, whole bodies floating. A girl's gone missing, plucked from your town close enough to the sea to sound like it: a rumbling hush of suspicion. Flash—a fish, and the pelican swooping. Your daughter knows that oceans explain what you can't: depth, distance, diagnosis that drifts you too far out. You leave her, you leave her, and then one day you'll leave her. When she asks each time you look her in the eye and lie.

Brought to Life

Did you know people sometimes use their tongues to kiss? she asks. It's
bedtime; she's lying on her back like Snow White you just read about, her
still lips red and waiting for the prince. When you're not shocked—the
second you grin *That's true*—your daughter wants to try it. She's almost
eight. You've seen the boys at recess pick her first. The one who you said
Yes to years ago made your name into a spell. Each night you lie beneath
him in the dark he whispers it. The part your daughter loves: when you
said *Yes*, he took you to another land. On the famous church's ceiling:
God looking down his outstretched arm, his finger reaching through
the air. You'd barely touched each other then. Your daughter puckers
up and points her tongue at you. In the painting, Adam waits. He's
there—though really, his life hasn't started yet. This is how she'll feel one
day. You're leaning in to her. You'll try to show your daughter how to love;
one day, she'll leave in search of someone else to care for her. In the deep
woods, then, your voice will be a tiny call that's lost. She'll question every
mirror until one answers, You.

The Day You Choose

You sit in the back. A woman in the movie suffers; her demon is one you can see. You pick through your pills by the light of her scream. The woman has been begging for help since this started. By now, she's alone. It's your story. You could fill a theater with those who don't get it. Two walk past you up the aisle. This has got to end soon, you think. On-screen, the woman who wanted to die has changed her mind.

"Give us the baby, give us the baby, throw us the baby"

—*New York Times*, 1-17-09

When my son calls, it's all about Survivorman: the show, the man who,
four days left and starving, dug deep holes for traps then stalked his
bait, who turned his camera on, put it in the bottom of one pit and
filmed straight up so those at home could see. Away for the first time,
my son notes how to live on his own. I'm the guy on TV: counting the
days, talking to myself, lying awake. Obsessing on what the body can't
survive without. Water: it caught the jet today. Everyone's okay. My son's
describing Survivorman's camera, the bright circle of blue it filmed, the
silence and the shifting sky—then he says *You can't believe what all of a
sudden fell in.* On the wing, a woman clutched her baby boy; the Hudson
rose around them. Though men on the lifeboat reached and screamed,
she wouldn't give him up. Of course she wouldn't give him up. I've seen
Survivorman not even last a week alone. I hold my son's voice like a rope.
He keeps on telling me just what it's like in the trap.

Recovery 6: The Last Word

Experts like to point out things that you can't see. The woman in a vest, Whale Watching Spoken Here, hands your son binoculars, aims him at the gray. The ocean breathes like a hospital machine. You've come here many times before, alone; each time, you've left discouraged: nothing there. The experts like to say *Have faith*. You prayed for years your pain would go away; for years, you said you're fine and prayed your son believed. *Keep an eye out for the blow*, the woman says. You turn: your son is watching you. Has been watching all along, you realize. You pull him close, wrap your coat around his back. The expert checks her chart and shakes her head. *Too bad*, she says. *You just missed the best time.* She fakes a frown. You're done with these people. You drop your head and whisper to your son *No—she has no idea*. You walk together toward the car, heads down in the rain like you're about to dive. Out there, a mother whale and her son begin their long swim north today. You know it will be slow, this mother leading her new life. You'll tell him everything. *Why now?* your son will ask and you'll say *Now the mother's strong enough.*

Notes

In "Name One Thing You Love," the lines *"beginning to be something/That no one has ever been and lived through"* are from James Dickey's poem "Falling."

The mountain town of Sapa, in "For Chloe, Whose Name Means 'Profusion of Blooms,'" is in northwest Vietnam, near the Chinese border, and is home to many ethnic minority groups.

The title "'Give us the baby, give us the baby, throw us the baby'" is taken from an article in the *New York Times* about the successful crash-landing of US Airways flight 1549 in the Hudson River.

Other Books in the Crab Orchard Series in Poetry

Muse
Susan Aizenberg

Lizzie Borden in Love:
Poems in Women's Voices
Julianna Baggott

This Country of Mothers
Julianna Baggott

The Sphere of Birds
Ciaran Berry

White Summer
Joelle Biele

In Search of the Great Dead
Richard Cecil

Twenty First Century Blues
Richard Cecil

Circle
Victoria Chang

Consolation Miracle
Chad Davidson

The Last Predicta
Chad Davidson

Furious Lullaby
Oliver de la Paz

Names above Houses
Oliver de la Paz

The Star-Spangled Banner
Denise Duhamel

Beautiful Trouble
Amy Fleury

Soluble Fish
Mary Jo Firth Gillett

Pelican Tracks
Elton Glaser

Winter Amnesties
Elton Glaser

Strange Land
Todd Hearon

Always Danger
David Hernandez

Red Clay Suite
Honorée Fanonne Jeffers

Fabulae
Joy Katz

DATE DUE

GAYLORD			PRINTED IN U.S.A.